THE BRADFORD COUNT

IAN DUHIG

The Bradford Count

BLOODAXE BOOKS

ISBN: 1 85224 138 1

First published 1991 by
Bloodaxe Books Ltd,
P.O. Box 1SN,
Newcastle upon Tyne NE99 1SN.

Bloodaxe Books Ltd acknowledges
the financial assistance of Northern Arts.

For Jane and Owen

Cover reproduction by V & H Reprographics, Newcastle upon Tyne.

Printed in Great Britain by
Billing & Sons Limited, Worcester.

*The man who loves his homeland
is a beginner; he to whom every soil
is as his own is strong; but he is
perfect for whom the entire world
is a foreign country.*

HUGH OF ST VICTOR

*You are impertinent, they said to me.
I'm not impertinent, I said: I'm lost.*

BRECHT: 'Emigrant's Lament'

Acknowledgements

A few of these poems, or some very like them, have already appeared elsewhere. Acknowledgements are therefore due to the editors of the following publications: *Ambit, Arion, Bête Noire, Bottlenose Review, The Dolphin, Foolscap, Fortnight, Gown, The Honest Ulsterman* (especially), *The Irish Review, New Statesman & Society, Oxford Poetry, Poetry & Audience, Rhinoceros, Sanity* and *The Times Literary Supplement.*

'Archbishop Mar Jacobus Remembers the Baron' appeared on a Bernard Stone /Turret Bookshop Poem Card. 'Splenditello' was among the joint winners of the 1989 Northern Poetry Competition, consequently appearing in its anthology *Northern Poetry One* (Littlewood Press, 1989). These last two poems will also form part of an exhibit in this year's Gay Pride Week show at the Old Museum Building, Belfast.

'Nineteen Hundred and Nineteen' won the 1987 National Poetry Competition and appeared in that competition's anthology from the Poetry Society, and was broadcast on Radio 3 and Radio Leeds as a result. 'The Irish Slave' was broadcast on the Radio Ulster programme *Readings from Garron Tower* in 1990. 'From the Plague Journal' won the 1989 *Sanity* Poetry Competition. And let's not forget Freddie and Fungie, without whose help none of these poems would have survived the attention of otters.

Contents

From the Irish

According to Dineen, a Gael unsurpassed
in lexicographical enterprise, the Irish
for moon means 'the white circle in a slice
of half-boiled potato or turnip'. A star
is the mark on the forehead of a beast
and the sun is the bottom of a lake, or well.

Well, if I say to you your face
is like a slice of half-boiled turnip,
your hair is the colour of a lake's bottom
and at the centre of each of your eyes
is the mark of the beast, it is because
I want to love you properly, according to Dineen.

Fundamentals

Brethren, I know that many of you have come here today
because your Chief has promised any non-attender
that he will stake him out, drive tent-pegs through his anus
and sell his wives and children to the Portuguese.
As far as possible, I want you to put that from your minds.
Today, I want to talk to you about the Christian God.

In many respects, our Christian God is not like your God.
His name, for example, is not also our word for rain.
Neither does it have for us the connotation 'sexual intercourse'.
And although I call Him 'holy' (we call Him 'Him', not 'It',
even though we know He is not a man and certainly not a woman)
I do not mean, as you do, that He is fat like a healthy cow.

Let me make this clear. When I say 'God is good, God is everywhere',
it is not because He is exceptionally fat. 'God loves you'
does not mean what warriors do to spear-carriers on campaign.
It means He feels for you like your mother or your father –
yes I know Chuma loved a son he bought like warriors
love spear-carriers on campaign – that's *Sin* and it comes later.

From today, I want you to remember just three simple things:
our God is different from your God, our God is better than your God
and my wife doesn't like it when you watch her go to the toilet.
Grasp them and you have grasped the fundamentals of salvation.
Baptisms start at sundown but before then, as arranged,
how to strip, clean and re-sight a bolt-action Martini-Henry.

Stolen Marches

Ó Riada cracking macaronic from his harpsichord:
'There's a place near Glen Feask – the Robber's Glen…'
The worn yarn of slaughtered yeomanry,
of horses and harness pitched in a bog.
A pause, then the clan march *Fead an Iolair*,
the Eagle's Whistle among the moths.

Major Maurice Meade (Munster Brigades)
our family friend, frightened me when I was small –
he slept with his eyes open – and when I asked
how it felt shooting tans or staters
he talked only of the uniforms he'd worn,
the dances he had been to.

'…*Tiarna Mhuigheo*, who was the boy to wrassle!'
Seditious amusement. Then Ó Sullivan's,
the warlord's march played like a slow jig
with Colonel de Buitléar guesting on accordion.
Damhsa, rinnce, words taken from enemies.
Irish has no word for dance.

Patriot Game

Being still attached to his cap
    after he was shot, his friends
who shot him buried it decently
    under the hawthorn by the old bath
horses came to drink from, until
    fearing that the pigs in their grief
would snuffle too long by its grave,
    they dug it up again themselves
and sent it to his other friends

who'd buried all the rest of him
    with a cortège of gun-carriages
borrowed from the mutual foe
    to shell the friends who shot him
(using the dumdum bullets
    stolen from the mutual foe)
which started this whole pantomime,
    him wearing that cap of his,
friends of his shooting at it.

Dybenko's Demob

When the Executive Committee of the Military-Revolutionary
    Tribunal of the Makhno Army
summoned a Fourth Extraordinary Convention of Peasants,
    Workers and Insurgents
at Guliay-Polie, Trotsky countered with Order 1824 of the
    Military-Revolutionary
Council of the Republic ('Rev-Com'), threatening referral of those
    in attendance
to the Provisional Committee of the Revolutionary Tribunal
    (being shot).

I preferred the Grishin Front. Go to the wrong meeting here –
they're all alike – you wind up in a Cheka cellar.
Fortunately, I am only interested in carp. Bloody great fat carp,
sodden with yoghurt. She whispers, 'Lenin will soon be dead;
triumvirates are forming!' 'Horseshit. Pass the carp.'

The Frog
(for Leon McAuley)

The ollamh faltered in his staves,
a gilly spilled his wine-cask:
the Ossory court circled a wonder;
'It is the living budget of The Morrígan!'
'It is the handsomest child of a Connachtman!'
'It is the ghost of a drunkard's stomach!'
'Without doubt, it's a Fomorian cat.'
'Without doubt, it's from Paddington.'
'Without doubt, it's an ugly bugger isn't it?'

The frog gulped, swivelled its headlamp eyes
and burped like an earl. The hall stilled,
its eyes fixed on Duvenold,
king and seer. He knew he must pronounce –
Warfare, Pestilence, the Gael in Chains –
that sort of thing. It was expected. 'Friends,'
he cried, 'this hare-fish means Death to Ireland;
Warfare, Pestilence, the Gael in Chains!
It also shags that poem of Muldoon's.'

The Irish Slave

It is the Night of Power and the puppeteers
are playing *Karaguez, Martyr to Chastity.*
Nubian grooms are breaking cameleopards.
Janissaries line their cloaks with lynx.

Sultan Mahmoud shows off his new French wife
on a caïque drawn by jewelled fish.
They fan the Bosphorus like a wedding train
with an escort of heartbroken gulls.

The pirates came down on Baltimore
like gulls to romp a bucket of fish-heads.
A traitor's black cross marked us on their maps;
they laid another black cross upon us.

The Kizlar Aga was all sympathy,
bruising almonds with myrrh for emulsions
and poultices of medicinal sand.
He told me it was either this or death.

At home I would have worn the priest's black frock
with the farm to Michael and Hugh abroad;
years of forgiving the sins of children
and women while men diced in the church porch.

Castration has been a good career move.
I will learn to call the nightingales bulbuls
I could be drinking my mother's badger tea;
the Kizlar is preparing my sherbet.

Vatsyayana called Mrillana Advises the Suitor

A man should pierce his lingam with sima-patra stalks
and clean the wound with liquorice and honey:
apadravyas may then be inserted of gold or ivory
or of such woods as bottle-gourd or teak. To taste,
these may be roughened into globules or shaped
according to traditional designs, as for example:
    armlet,
    double-armlet,
    round on one side,
    round,
    the flower,
    wooden mortar,
    bone of the heron,
    goad of the elephant,
    the collection of eight balls,
    where four roads meet.

Sundry Receipts of Vatsyayana called Mrillana written in the form of Sutra

The black pigment produced by grinding the burned bone
of a hawk or kite with antimony and brushed
under the eyelashes gives power over men.

Lac wetted seven times in sweat from the testicles
of a white horse will brighten the lip.
The lip may be darkened by chewing madayontikas.

Juice of cassia, jambolana and veronia,
thickened with powdered lohopa-jihirka,
destroys love when smeared on a woman's yoni.

Congress with a woman bathed in the stale milk
of buffaloes, garlic and hog-plum
dried with thorn-apple works to like effect.

A paste of milk-hedge, myrabolons, kuili
and monkey-excrement thrown over a woman
against a golden moon will keep her faithful.

A woman who comes near a man playing bagpipes
dressed with juice of vajra, the urine of hyena
and goat-butter will be disgusted by him.

A man garlanded with asparagus, jasmine,
blue lotus and the sloughed skins of cobras
will be the source of endless conversation.

Shlakshnaparni, worn while hunting tiger
alone, unarmed, on foot, by moonlight,
is a certain cure for constipation.

Seeds of pomegranate and cucumber
ground to an ointment with ghee and arabicus
are, to my knowledge, completely useless.

After Poggio
(1380-145?)

Rodi's Accommodation

Antonio Rodi, the Minorite Priest,
saying mass at Jesi in Piceno –
a town of most sceptical peasants –
announced as his sermon's theme: 'The Christ,

Who Fed Five Hundred on Crusts.' 'Thousand,' hissed
his clerk, 'He fed five thousand!' 'Die on a sword!'
snapped back Rodi, desperate in his plight,
'Even now they hardly believe a word!'

The Battle Sermon

'Kill for God and Florence, and if you die,'
the Greek cardinal exhorted his pikes,
'If you die, know you dine with God tonight!'
Riding past the rearguard he met some Greeks

hired from Venice by the White Ghibelline.
They called, 'Dodging God's supper, Cardinal?'
'Yes, icon-makers, when Tuscans squabble
over seats they drench everyone with wine.'

Civic Duties

A Venetian and a Florentine,
waiting to denounce Peace-Speakers
before the Court of Morals, bickered
about the excise on each other's wine,

access to the sea, the Milanese Pact:
'Florence fights only that Florence might be free!'
'Free from debt and and honour! Milan is weak.
Our common cause is made on treachery.'

*In this war it was made a capital offence
to be heard speaking of peace in Florence.*

Sport with a Servant

A company of Florentine Merchants
were sharing wine and tomacelli
at the palace of Cardinal della Bari.
Guessing for the famous new incarnations –

Ridolfo as goat, Dante as termite –
for sport, they asked a servant of the house
a shape for Lorenzo. 'A melon,' he smiled,
'You all queue now to smell his arse!'

*In Florence they test a melon's
freshness by smelling its rear end.*

Proverbs

Alto the Mad was playing on his flute –
'Hanging from the Noose' as the Romans say –
when the evening wind bore down the reeds
about his feet. 'No homage pay to me

masters of Rome. I am the least among you!'
sang Alto, who again began playing.
A child then burst his kidney with a stone.
His last words too are now a Roman saying.

A Crippling Jealousy

Giovanni Andrea, Bolognese doctor,
famous far beyond that great city's walls
wished proof of his wife's illicit affair
so hid her brevet and cut off his balls.

*A brevet is a charm of virgin thread worn by women
commonly as a prophylactic against conception.*

The Last Ass

Bonaccio Guasci bore corn to Fighino
packed on his six best asses. He rode one home,
thus counting only five about him
as they shuffled into his piazza.

His wife, who at that moment groaned under
Cardinal della Bari, cried in her bliss:
'O the mountains seem to fall before me!'
Bona called, 'Whistle if you see my last ass!'

The Strength of Genoa

Francesco Quartente, Florentine trader,
latterly came to dwell in Genoa.
A neighbour there, Nigniaccia,
scoffed at his thin son, his thinner daughter.

'A Florentine trader must work on his own,'
he granted. 'We lack the brotherhood of you
Genoese sailors, who when your wives spawn,
have had the help of the entire ship's crew.'

Omen

This month, winds shattered Borgeto Castle,
St Rufino's Abbey on the Tiber
and many farms. Keystones were crushed to chaff,
campaniles snapped like reeds; ox-drivers

saw the dead cardinal in Easter vestments
elbow through the thunderclouds and tear
the Government's Watchtower from its base.
Of this, time will grant intelligence.

* * *

Margery Kempe's

Beneath her white wool pilch, the trial hair shirt
she cut from malt-nets rotted with her tears.
Her husband later burned their kiln in rage
when he grasped what she meant by cleanliness.

While suffragans grilled her for Lollardry,
gnawed her visions like rats gnawing stockfish,
she prayed to St Mary of Antioch
who exploded the dragon which ate her.

The pilgrim's shell instructed her in tongues
miraculously strange to every land.
In Jerusalem she learned how to scream
and was roasted for Flagellantism.

She returned with the bull for the church font,
with dreams of a bear which gorged on blossom
and farted petal-storms over priestly spies.
Her neighbours called this the cheese parable.

Tap the ribs of this her burned-out poem
as she tapped the dovecote of Christ's body,
you'll cry with sootfalls from a brewing-kiln,
with falling dust, scales and white, white feathers.

Darkly

Through the glass of his waterclock
Konrade of Megenburg reflected on
the weeping crocodiles of torchlight
that crawled between his mullions.
They filed before the market cross
then fell; adulterers face-down,
liars on one side, three fingers raised
as if signalling the hymn –
"Had it not been for our contrition
All Christendom had met Perdition!"
What he'd mistook for rosaries were whips.

'This plague is of promiscuous effect;
it cannot therefore be God's work'
he scratched in his *Buch der Natur*
to cries and the noise of stoning.
"Mercy ye ne'er to others show
None shall ye find but endless woe!"
'Some blame the Jews which is illogic;
their Viennese dead put out the stars:
our true light is the open mind.'
The clock dipped. He threw fists of aloes,
calamite and storax on the open fire.

I would physic these wretched hale
with piss-a-bed for their wit's cachexia,
with spikenard for their loathings.
Post equitem sedet atra cura –
it's Man hitches and burrs the saddle.
Here we spit the moneylenders:
Cyprus burns its Arab slaves.
Smoke blinds the Virgin's loving eyes:
we waste the best that plague preserves
and herb true-love will not restore it
nor hedge-mustard recover one lost voice.

Splenditello

1

I, Guliano Carlini, third richest man
in Vellano, this scurf-edge of the Apennines,
where our children are assailed by witches
in the shapes of swallows or nightingales,
which is rich only in undowried girls,
which is scoffed at even in Pescia,
I do promise and avow, Madonna,
that I will make my house a shrine to you,
and my only child, my daughter Benedetta,
blessed, will be herself a hymn to you,
whose long birth that midwife is now botching
because she has lain with seven devils
and as a midwife will, a wetnurse will,
so by my own hand I will raise her, Madonna,
but intercede for me with Christ your son,
loosen the cord from Benedetta's neck
that she may be delivered soon, breathing,
and later sing your mercy and His charity
in the best convent I can afford
where she will be commended with St Jerome's words:
'If a woman is for toil and childbirth
she is further than soul from body to a man.
If she would then serve Christ more than this world
she is no more a woman, and will be called a man.'

2

When Benedetta married Jesus Christ
He designed the ceremony Himself;
the green altar-cloth referred to her hope,
red silk flowers to her love, blue brocade
to the exertion of her mind on Paradise.
Twelve gloves represented the Apostles
and thirty-three candles His earthly years
('And buy the best wax! not those stumps of lard
you smoked out the chapel with last Easter!')

the largest three were banded twice with gold
for His charity and the Madonna's mercy.
The mud floor symbolised the rest of us.

But it was always me, poor Bartolomea
who was there for her night-sweats and visions
and Bartolomea who held her palms
when they shot blood into her silkworking,
Bartolomea who pressed down His Sacred Heart
when it slid about her ribcage like a loaf,
who softened for her that graceless movement
in her genuflection, who smuggled in
the Cremonese mortadella He had banned,
who was loved by Christ or Satan with her body.
Christ. Satan. They all piss in the same pot.

3

'Dear Christ, to make a mountain goat Abbess!'

'She could read, keep the books, was good for business –
much was harmless; a saffron ring, foil stars,
some self-inflicted wounds, a few visions...'

'Visions, or the mists from a woman's heat?'

'The *Liber Gomorrhianus* is silent on that
(as you know is Dante). No instruments were used.
They call it 'the mute sin'. Fillucio
ranks it minor, as does Sinistrari...'

'So neither sodomy nor blasphemy
will burn her. I suppose she did marry...'

'...albeit above herself. We are come
above all to crush an embarrassment,
so we cite Aquinas with Bartolomea
and press for St Theresa's solution.'

'Agreed. Solitary confinement until death.'

Most Honourable Abbess, this respectful note
is borne by Piera, my eldest daughter,
for whom my family cherish the hope
that your kindness will accept her to your convent.
You will understand, therefore, that if I mention
the fifty scudi outstanding on your account
it is that I may return it to you
as dowry. However, that is not to the point.

Last night as I set about repairing
the last delivery of sister's clogs
with the very best of my new alder
cut and shaped by myself with the new growth
from the north bank of the river Arno,
I fixed one hardly-worn pair to the lasts
and brushed down the soles to inspect the wear,
for I am not one of these clog-menders
that puts new soles on good clogs, for I know
the style of young women who trip and slur their feet,
and that it is your duty before Christ,
who is not taken in by sinners in good shoes,
to keep a hold upon expenditure.
But forgive my rambling, I am an old man
with too many daughters and begging your pardon.

What I had not seen with my weak eyes
was revealed to me by the mud left after brushing,
caught in the shallowest of etchings on each heel.
They were designs of the most exquisite beauty;
on the left a swallow in flight over
an antique landscape which, continued on the right,
showed a nightingale, its tiny beak wide
and the bird rendered so delicately
that all my family later dreamt of its song.
It must have been worked with the finest of burins –
a diamond perhaps, or a sliver of glass.
Piera, who is well read and polite
(and hard-working into the bargain) has told me
they represent Philomela's nightingale
and the swallow of Procne, two women
like our Martha and Mary, who loved the same man.

It honours your sisters and St Augustine's Rule
that such a divine prayer to the service of Christ
is forced from the action of mud. Abbess,
if it pleases you Piera could take your veil
even today, clearing your honourable debt
and earning my unrepayable gratitude.
Her goods and gifts for you are waiting at the shrine.
I know the Madonna will guide your decision.

Hosts

Had Mary Riordan been Egyptian
she would have sautéed *Blaps mortisaga*
with honey, butter and sesame oil,
but suffering is the share of the Gael:
Mary drank the eggs of churchyard beetles
in her pious soup of dew from priests' graves.
These thrived on transubstantiated hosts
(shovelled down for Mary's Easter Duty)
and she brought up theophagous larvae
every mass till pressure from the clergy
forced the girl to dose with turpentine.
She nursed ulcers when the grubs aborted,
but kept a pink fragrance to her urine
according to scientific experts
like Dr John Hunter, the man who burked
the Irish Giant of his skeleton.
Until his fiancée laid the law down,
his colonies of syphilis on grafts
lifted from the corpse of a prostitute
burned across his body like a famine.

The Lady Who Loved Insects

Yatai Bayashi is the Festival of Drums:
men beat Taikos through the night;
KODŌ (Children of the Drum) KODŌ (Heartbeat);
but I danced Nishimonai to bones,
ground chalk for my breasts, gallstone
for my teeth, for I was twelve and marriageable.

For the Perfume Contest I chose
Grape-and-Cherry brocade over simple
cotton trousers; mixed aloes
with cinammon and tulip for wine-breath,
conch to mask the candlesmoke and sweet-pines
for memory. I won the Jijū and Genjī, my Shining Prince.

His morning poem was a disappointment −
life in his shinden worse. He bored me with pillow-books,
gossamer diaries, his healthy attitude to sex.
He thought me too good at Chinese for a woman
and beat me when I capped his verses.
I murdered him by the cinder garden.

No one sees my face now. My maids gossip
or get drunk. They say I am possessed by foxes
because I won't take lovers. 'Ghosts and women,'
I whisper through the screens, 'are best invisible.'
My "novels" astonish the Fujiwara. They send me gifts
of paper, and cicadas with gilded wings.

The Badly-Loved
(for Patricia Mallon)

Apollinaire

No man was good enough to be my father;
the Registrar of Bastards being up to D
my mother called me Kostrowitzky,
but at Neuglück hard by the Seven Mountains,
downstream from the miraculous head
I became its namesake, the poet that I am.
Neuglück! The fish-skinned Vicomtesse designed it,
her pumpernickel velvety with ergot, the day
her father's boarhounds ate their dolls-house.
She loved me deeply, as did they all,
but I had chosen the English governess
with her Virgin-of-the-Bean blue eyes,
those eye-pods the colour of Egyptian lentils
and that mouth, a royal barge of Carthage
flaming behind the white cities of her teeth.
Our words poured like honey from a madman's tongue,
pledges of the flesh redeemed by starlight.
At times I left her speechless with my dash –
as on Drachenfels where Siegfried conquered.
She was all *Yes, Yes* on the precipice
but down among the accordions and Rhenish tenors
barking roundelays for chopping sauerkraut
her nerve failed. My love died like her eyes
and I strode forward, master of my voice.

Annie

I remember the secretary's pear-shaped skull
always in a cloud of shag – smoking a narcisse,
his chest whistled like a pan of shellfish –
but it is the Countess I'll never forget!
She was sporting black then for Count Unicorn,
who'd earned his name for one outstanding cyst,
while her daughter knocked some corners off the Greek

lined up to fill his slippers. We pitied Kostro
with his damp hands and flat, beseeching cheekbones:
like my father, his voice seemed to come from his neck.
Men are such dummies. I'd walk him for her
where the wind took his smoke and endless French –
I didn't speak it, which certainly helped.
Once, though, I'm sure he suggested we should marry.
I felt hunted. *We?* I kept repeating, *We?*
So did he, which really got on my nerves,
especially during the harvest concert.
I could have cheerfully cut off his head.
About that time I chose to live abroad,
somewhere far, somewhere beginning with A.
Barring once in the earthquake I've never wavered.
Now you come with talk of Kostro's poetry,
of Beatrice and Laura – my name is Annie,
and I'd like to hear about the Countess' daughter.

Another Poem About Old Photographs

This one's good. Look closely, you can almost
detect each ridge and whorl of Uncle Tommy's index-
fingerprint. That white curved edge top left – that's
the sky we had in Cork, Nineteen Fifty-Six,

the summer of his first box-camera. This one
I call 'Late Malevich: Town Hall, Macroom',
or, if in a figurative whimsy, 'Klansmen
Routed by Doves in Freak Arkansas Snowstorm'.

It should have been the family group
but Tommy was, by then, flouting convention.
Drunk with Kodakry, he'd wave us round, then swoop –
Duhigs trapped between his cross-sights and the sun,

the Red-faced Baron, hunched behind a black box
which struggled to record his flights of art
on sun-bleached or thumb-benighted film. This next
came out. My Mother couldn't believe it.

Plain as sin, my Father's Harris blocks the view
to Gougane Barra from Glengariff Bay.
'The best jacket I ever had,' he'd say,
'No doubt about it. The camera doesn't lie.'

I'r Hen Iaith A'i Chaneuon

'If the tongue only speak all that the mind knows
There wouldn't be any neighbours' – THE RED BOOK OF HERGEST

When I go down to Wales for the long bank holiday
to visit my wife's grandfather who is teetotal,
who is a non-smoker, who does not approve
of anyone who is not teetotal and a non-smoker,
when I go down to Wales for the long, long bank holiday
with my second wife to visit her grandfather
who deserted Methodism for The Red Flag,
who won't hear a word against Stalin,
who despite my oft-professed socialism
secretly believes I am still with the Pope's legions,
receiving coded telegrams from the Vatican
specifying the dates, times and positions I should adopt
for political activity and sexual activity,
who in his ninetieth year took against boxing,
which was the only thing I could ever talk to him about,
when I visit my second wife's surviving grandfather,
and when he listens to the football results in Welsh
I will sometimes slip out to the pub.

I will sometimes slip out to the pub
and drink pint upon pint of that bilious whey
they serve there, where the muzak will invariably be
The Best of the Rhosllanerchrugog Male Voice Choir
and I will get trapped by some brain donor from up the valley
who will really talk about 'the language so strong and so beautiful
that has grown out of the ageless mountains,
that speech of wondrous beauty that our fathers wrought,'
who will chant to me in Welsh his epileptic verses
about Gruffudd ap Llywellyn and Daffydd ap Llywellyn,
and who will give me two solid hours of slaver
because I don't speak Irish and who will then bring up religion,
then I will tell him I know one Irish prayer about a Welsh king
on that very subject, and I will recite for him as follows:
'Na thracht ar an mhinisteir Ghallda
Na ar a chreideimh gan bheann gan bhrí,
Mar ni'l mar bhuan-chloch da theampuill
Ach magairle Annraoi Rí.' 'Beautiful,'
He will say, as they all do, 'It sounds quite beautiful.'

Rural Drives

1 *The Rustic Gigolo*

It's running round the front to kiss them
I hate. That and the risk of hookworm.

2 *The Fancy*

Go for the yard boss, the greedy chuck shy
of hens. Red birds show spine, that's the story.
Feed him dry manchet spiced with aniseed,
wood sorrel and boiled best wine. Dawns only.
Hot him young but every night bathe the spurs
in salt and whisky. Crop the wattle, quills
and pare one half-inch from the lower beak
for grip and attack. Keep him well-blooded
but spoil all the kills – he'll be mad for one
when you back him with hard money. Starve him
the dawn of his first fight. Score his gaffles
their length with old nails – they work like blood-grooves
and harbour rust. After, pack his gashes
with butter and rosemary, his eye-wounds
with pads of alehoof dampened in cold tea.
Even whipped he must make it to the scratch
in three minutes. Or give him to your dog.

3 *The Country Churchyard*

This wraps it up. It would appear,
from these despatches in marble,
the price of falling asleep here
is immediate burial.

The Green Man's Cat

*'And the unfed cat toys with the yin-yang of a tennis ball,
debating whether* yes *is* no' – CIARAN CARSON

I gave a Kawasaki tennis racket
to my love, who kissed me then hit the ceiling;
'It's made in Korea and it's made from *whale!*'
Abashed, my gaze sank on Balthasar the cat
shaking the moustache he'd bitten from its strings,
so she gave him a piece of her mind as well.

That midnight I picked my way between his teeth
snagged with fluke and broken net, a piece of mind,
trailing a clue to the string question (its length),
and though his great tongue heaved like Leviathan,
and his throat purred up a thunder-harp of wind,
it sounded like nothing so much as nothing.

There was a silence at his thirty-eighth breath
which lasted no longer than the moment
a fisherman sees wealth in his harpoon-sight
and that was all, that was the complete koan.
I couldn't see it convincing Juliet;
I decided on a pantomime instead.

I paint across my t-shirt, 'When you say no,
it sounds just like a Korean saying *yes!*'
and screw a coin, one for each word, in my eyes
then jump her. She hits the moon; 'I get *nothing*,'
she's snarling, '*Nothing* from you but *parlour tricks!*'
I say nothing, a sphinx to my broken nose.

The Bradford Count

Marshall's fingers blurred in the kemp,
frisking its staple for the Bradford Count.
He set it with the Dalesbreds
grazing his mill's glass roof.

His Jacob's Sheep at Bolton Abbey chew over the bones
of the Lord Secretary of Ireland – a talented man,
stabbed for his trouble. I fed them Boland
biscuits in a partisan gesture. Later, in Skipton

I bought this plate: a face like Marshall's,
perhaps, or Cavendish; fringed with dog-rose
and crowned a shamrock-laurelled 'Erin Go Bragh'.
'Parnell,' I told her, 'Parnell. Rhymes with "carnal".'

Nobby the Nubian choked on his beard. I buried
his hide in old tea-leaves and made a bodhrán.
You might call me 'Heartless', or 'Skin-the-Goat'.
But I honour him, twice, in my fashion.

A Scarborough Warning

'Otaheite, that fallen Paradise...'
CHARLES DARWIN
Zoology of the Voyage of the 'Beagle'

Rise, Curator Stackpole of Mystic,
where Dissenters fixed their bride-prices
in dolphin-meat: join us Beaglehole,
scholar of the dreamtime murderers,
we'll swing in the *Resolution*'s wake
with luck like Mother Carey's Chickens.

Below us now Cook's Whitby collier
still beats on to that hourglass landfall,
its crew's bellies reefed with sauerkraut,
their Fearnought jackets hemmed with brass nails.
It is flying fish weather, killing heat.
The flags translate like a Scarborough Warning.

Tonight we must spring the oubliette
on Hodges, who painted this island
first in oils, then worked in banks; Burnett
'whose every act proves him a woman';
Séan Marra, his shoulderblades flogged out
and blinking like the mountain butterflies.

Tonight they grill us for all we know:
D'où venons-nous? Stackpole gutters dumb.
Qui sommes-nous? Beaglehole coughs feathers.
Où allons-nous? in Tahitian please!
'Your definite article was O...'
Was O. My palate is burning with lime.

Fatras Baton

The sugar falls like black snow on Noé
by where Mackandal the Poisoner
was burnt and burst from his stake.

Napoleon's new Commissioner,
the insane Sonthonax, is white
and incites d'occos to slaughter whites.

Our Black Spartacus, L'Ouverture,
protects us, but grows smoky-haired with age.
(Napoleon has marked him for exile).

The English say we French must like burnt sugar
in our coffee. I toast their officers
from our very best Jacobite glass.

My darling, I write under a bad turn of the moon.
Kiss the children for me. If I should not return
claim compensation. Burn the punishment books.

The Cat and Banjo

He lit his cigar with the last crested telegram,
drifting blue ash over the stinkwood davenport.
The sundry debtors ledger curled like the brim
of a smasher hat. 'If was the master.
Played the cat and banjo with my heart.
Words can't...bad as Majuba.' Now Doornkop
was teaching his codebooks to speak Dutch.
Table Mountain boomed across the stoep.
He snapped his glass from the poet's sketch
of some raiding ape neck-deep in esparto,
its great head framed by whiskey-cusps,
its very species a smudged graffito.

King of Infinite Space

He slammed the coins king-down on the counter
for his five-thousandth bottle of champagne,
marking off another life's ambition.
Shelved himself in Varzin, Old Egg-Dancer,
scrambler of telegrams, Prince Iron Mouth
souses nights whitened by hate with Black Velvet –
another brilliant union: Gallic froth
Borussianised by porter; civet
in steins. He'd roll out herring-salted tears
at all the nightmares coming sure as trains
slamming along tracks cindered by the bones
of whom? Pomeranian grenadiers?

Asmodeus

When I drank New Jersey Champagne
with Edgar Allan Poe I'd tell the boys
to lace his heavy with the turnip juice
and it was Edgar *A.* Poe *not* Allan
to his face. I knew he could be touchy
as a flayed man – folk called him 'Tomahawk'
from the edge on his tongue – even Eddy
'd do when he came down the Bowery
as he liked to, for our dancing music.
Now the Daybreak Boys liked the Irish stuff
but Lee-Annabel's stood on Roach Guard turf
and they called all the tunes. That meant one week
the 'Ethiopian Delineators'
who swapped with the 'Dixie Melodeers',
but 'bourine, bones, banjo and the fiddle
could play a blackface Irish just as well
and Eddy'd dance with a twelve-year-old mab
and talk about the Throne of Solomon.
He'd say this jammed down some Beelzebub
under pillars of rubies and diamonds
and on its six gold steps sat twelve gold lions
and eagles shielded the eyes of Solomon
and seven doors opened onto his throne.
Now Eddy's stock came from Virginia
and he'd a wife die called Virginia
so he didn't hold with Abolition,
he'd cry: 'The Black Man has to be kept down
like Asmodeus under Solomon!
In the English use of our English tongue
the very term "Black Man" means The Daemon!'
He never seemed to notice I was black
(although not black like negro men are black)
or that his morals undermined his logic.
We knew the poor sap was wrong in the head,
but he was someone we could understand.
Us resurrection men can't waste a friend.
We knew the value of the truly dead.

On the Trail

'Christ goes deeper than I do, but I have wider experience'
FRANK HARRIS

In the green lamplight under the East River
Irish sandhogs talked of cattle-raids and queens,
whether Hickock could outfox Conchobar
or the terror of the bends and its visions.

The hotel cattletramps taught him ranch-brands
and changing them, to file a trigger-action
so a woman's touch would loose all five rounds,
Sioux cures for premature ejaculation

and the picture-songs of the Ojibwas
when the bootblacks shared their marijuana.
Then Frank dreamed of the Sacred Band of Thebes
buried miles from Schliemann's dig in Chaeroneia,

of Rhodes signing his telegrams 'The Women
of Johannesburg'. He turned from his own future
as from the raw vision of Emma Goldman
who'd sell herself for the price of a revolver.

Tanizaki of *The Discourse on Shadows* Demonstrates a Tokugawa Proverb

Harada O-kinu of the Storm in the Night
was a cherry in fresh leaf, and her shaved brow-line
borrowed violet from an edge of the rainbow
the day she was sold to a pawnbroker.
She redeemed herself, shaving raw bamboo
with his wild rice. The son of Osaka,
as I say, ruined himself because of food.

The Meiji headsman served Takahashi O-den
with his cutter's bill. She had killed for brocade-debt,
her lover's, but in Yanaka Cemetery,
honoured at last, her haiku cut in stone,
he left her. A public lavatory
stands by her grave. The son of Kyoto,
as I say, ruined himself with finery.

Hanai O-ume is a theatre woman
who plays herself. Catch her show at the old godown:
the geisha life; her dream of business; saving;
a pimp eyeing her in the new teahouse...
It was by willows and gently raining
when she cut his lights. The son of Edo,
so I'm told, ruined himself with his looking.

Archbishop Mar Jacobus Remembers the Baron

Even the Syro-Chaldean bishopric I offered
on the strength of *Hadrian the Seventh*
did not tempt Corvo. As mere Provost
to the Lieutenant of Grandmagistracy
of Sanctissima Sophia he fled
to Venice, convinced the Rhodes Trustees
were plotting his assassination.
Where else should provide a home
to the inventor of submarine photography?
I missed his inch-thick cigarettes,
gigantic Waterman fountain pens
and Graecocorvine vocabulary.
We played duets but kissed only once.
At last, he denounced me as a fraud
and schismatic. I said he played the spinet
like a lobster trying to escape its pot –
after that, my overtures were useless.
For all his violence and absurdity
I warm to think of him now,
his cropped grey hair dyed with henna,
his white hand wearing the spur-rowel ring
I gave him as defence against Jesuits
Closed round the oar of his panther-skinned gondola
diapered with crabs and ravens and flying
St George and the red and gold Vesilla
of the Bucintro Rowing Club.
I think less of the lagoon-eyed fauns
he photographs and masturbates.
Does he think of me in Godless Middlesex
where it either rains or they're playing cricket?
The Syro-Chaldean Church is not doing well
despite my sigils, blazons, banners
and the undeniable splendour of our ritual.
The landlord's wife is singing 'Auld Lang Syne'.
This is going to be a Godless century.

Nineteen Hundred and Nineteen

Dismissed from Tlaltizapa for changing sex
Manuel Palafox sulked in Arenista. At markets
he bought chimoyas, limes and ink from Oaxtepec.
Some days he wore his twenty-ounce sombrero,
deerskin pants and "charro" boots. On others
gold-embroidered blouses and red kerseymere skirts.

He wrote to Magonistas: 'Zapata is finished.
He takes orders from Obregon. Rally the Peones!
Death to Carranza! Tierra y Libertad!'
He wrote to Lenin: 'Trotsky is finished.
Seek concord with the Ukraine Makhnovshchina.
Brest-Litovsk's a cock-up. Regards to the Missus.'

He wrote to Freud: 'Were you coked when you dreamt up this?
No Mexican has even heard of the sexual revolution.
All Eros last year now it's Thanatos, bloody Thanatos.
Jung was right – grow a beard, you think you're Moses.
I hope your jaw drops off. Regards to the Missus.'
At last he wrote to Yeats: 'Dear Willie, how's the Vision?

Mine's double, ha-ha. Shit. Willie, I'm finished
in Mexico – it's full of bigots. Ireland can't be worse.
I'll work. Your brother paints – I'll hold his ladders.
You can have my poems. The one about this year –
change it round – it'll do for Ireland. What happened
to my lift with Casement? Willie, GET ME OUT OF HERE!'

Shopping in Cashel for pulque, Michael Robartes –
'Research Assistant to a popular writer' –
itched in his Connemara Cloth. Himself well-known
for a Special Devotion to the Virgin of Guadaloupe,
he frowned on local talk of a drunken madwoman
in red skirts, publicly disputing with the bishop.

So What Do You Think About Joyce?

While the night hours chimed from St Sepulchre's Without
Marcel Faugeron, the German Spy, raised his eyes,
his tin mug of whiskey, his Russian cigarette
and smiled at the judas-hole. Henry weighed up
this atheist Breton, rehearsing his prayers,
and marked three inches more to the Home Office Drop.

Naming the morning's parts – cap, noose, pin, lever, drop –
he dressed the wash-leather sleeve with castor oil,
brushed oil round its steel eye and waxed the pinion-strap –
cap, noose, dismiss assistant, pinion, lever, drop.
On the first stroke of eight he'd knock at the cell,
by the eighth, Marcel would have sunk his last drop.

At a loose end, Henry made a shift of pobs
from skinny prison milk and limy London bread.
The cooks sniggered at him: 'We get dronk in pobs
and we fish for pikelets. No it ain't spice-cake.
It comes from bleeding Dundee not bleeding Bradford.'
He read *Thomson's Weekly News* until daybreak

And his claim forms on the Scotch Mail. He'd been dry
since Mountjoy, when he'd needed his revolvers,
but by Leeds he was 'dronk', high as Gilderoy
and lost in a row with an Irish squaddie
enlisted with the King's Own Scottish Borderers
about hanging Joyce or the spelling of whiskey.

Lumpenhund

My torturer's hair smells of fallen leaves,
the times my family gathered acorns
for coffee. Evenings I'd stalk the wharves
so my paper clothes could smell of copra,
my wooden shoes not sound like poverty.

     One night I saw a shooting star
fall between the coamings on a steamer,
like a knot of kerosene-soaked oakum
falling from the hand of a saboteur.
To be on the safe side I joined them both.

My torturer's eyes are blank as the eggs
(which must be a fresh clutch of wild hen's eggs)
that transfer visa-stamps from one passport
to the next perfectly, if newly-boiled
and rolled warm on the feathery pages.

     One night I saw a shooting star
tumble between the bars of a gutter,
like some crumpled poem with name on name
written in lemon juice between its lines.
Finally my left hand denounced my right.

My torturer's hands are suppler
than the leather he soaks in egg-water
like a folk-cure, so he won't catch my warts.
Sparks are falling from my hair. I've confessed
to everything but the hunger.

Reforma Agraria

In 1936,
Falange or Carlist priests
showed wounded men,
republicans,
rojoseperatistas,
an extreme unction,
a cristazio limpio,
a blow with the crucifix
between the eyes,
a blessed paseo,
the light oil of the gun
like watchmaker's oil,
or sunflower oil,
ran from the Lugers,
ran from Berettas
down into the eyes
of wounded land-leaguers,
who closed them knowing
even then they'd won
two square metres,
room for the red rose tree.

From the Plague Journal

I have been asked to write about our food.

I remember nights spent hulling ration-rice,
soya beans pressed dry before they got to us,
boiling black-market sweetfish to hide their smell
from our Neighbourhood Monitor. We ate everything;
reed-root, pigweed, tugwort, bar-weed –
these may not be the scientific names.
We smuggled grated radish and bracken-sprouts
past our Neighbourhood Monitor once he started fainting,
propped beneath his Government banderoles:
    'There's Always Space to Plant a Pumpkin!'
    'The War is Only Just Beginning!'

Later our food became medicine:
dried fig-grubs for the incontinence;
ant-lions in saké for the headaches;
leek-leaves and cucumber for the burns.
I sold my son's thousand-stitch belt
for peaches and eggs which I mashed and strained,
mashed and strained. Still my children died,
the last little Tadashi setting his weasel-traps
of bamboo and abalone shells round the pond
he'd stocked with a few tiny carp fry.

That is all I remember about our food.

A Café Waiter in Tel Aviv

'O to be a café waiter in Tel Aviv!' – KAFKA

'We did not come from Russia to mix with blacks
or listen to their nigger-music!' 'Kurdish,'
whispered the guitarist, 'Perhaps it should be kaddish.'
His knife flicked open – the bar doors slammed shut.
'Drinks, waiter, I have made your café
Judenrein. Perhaps Hitler could have used me.'
'For shame, guitarist, you are still a Jew.'
'I'm told. But let me tell some things to you;

round Kraków my grandfather dug white lime,
practised Pilpul till the Tartar pogrom.
He fled west for Mendelssohn's Haskalah,
wed an Ashkenazi and taught High German
for low pay. Old Zvi met Marx – you know
his *On the Jewish Question*? "Money
is the God of Israel. The exchange-token
is the Jealous God of the Jew."

In 1933 Papa also learned:
"Framing these codes I have kept before me
the laws of Ezra and Nehemiah."
Thus spoke the drafter of the Nuremberg
Race Purity Laws. You know the rest –
boots in the night; the family dispersed.
I worked Rothschild's vineyards in Algeria
with Yemenite Jews, Jews from Libya.

"It is not more land we need, but more Jews!"
Ben-Gurion cried. We were smuggled in
by night, like arms, stashed in the maabaras,
the transit camps. Russian Jews had barracks
with bunks and stoves and portraits of Stalin.
We slept in sacks and dug hollows for our hips.
They bussed us round to break up Arab strikes,
harass their wives at market, burn their crops.

Papa did not approve my new career.
I left "resettlement" for the guitar.
I'm told Bialik, our "Russian–Hebrew
Poet" hates Arabs because they're like black Jews.
Tell me, I don't understand literature,
is this wit or something we should believe?'
'I'll tell you you'll be tried for such chatter.
I'm not a writer. This is Tel Aviv.'

Croix-des-Bouquets, Haiti

Most were naked but for the locked tin masks
which stop them sucking the cane they harvest.
We could see they had been made tigerish

by their whippings. Our sabres stuck in bone,
our saddle-girths were slashed by their children,
crones tore shot from the mouths of primed cannon

while our powder-monkeys fumbled and wept.
But we have laid them up in lavender.
They think their dead will wake in Africa.

A Squeeze
(for Adrian Rice)

'*Cork*, not York thank God!' I told the ticket-man,
like Mrs Knox, the Lady of my Quest,
so I'm in York boycotting its Mysteries
with their red-neck Jesus, their Jew-baiting text.

She was not in the Orange Gallery
where Lowry's *Clifford's Tower* could ignite its wall
had his white not dropped to bitter almond,
the green set off its blood-fused reveal.

About its ramps his ghostly figures fret:
'What is our motivation? Vengeance? Terror?
Or simply to give scale?' They beg transfer
to *Election Time, Going to the Match*

or even *Something Wrong*. I'd free them
but the painter's angry breath blows me past
the Minster, festive with St Elmo's fire,
to a red-roofed hostel for the homeless

and my Beatrice, pure white with weeping:
'They burned me out – so much was politics
but what of the Tailor? What of Ansty?
Bigots wedged their cabin-jamb with kindling

because their book was banned and burned, because
they knew cows from bulls, truths from traders' winds,
because the old woman was terrified by fire.'
And her tears dropped down like bitter almonds.

We hug her close, her teddy-bear and me,
whispering the Tailor's words of power:
'The whole world is only a blue bag:
Knock a squeeze from it whenever you can.'

To 'The March' from *Oscar and Malvina*
the Lady, her bear, Lowry's refugees,
me on Boru's Original Jews'-harp,
circle Clifford's whited gazebo

and knock down the walls of that birdless pile
and raise the seven-branched candelabra
to light up our dark cities, Ireland,
England, Europe, the whole blue bag.

The War

He has no face, Tatunciu,
in the club's dazzling footlights
but a child's voice, Farouk's
silhouette in white sharkskin
and gold identity bracelets:
'the war...everything. I was...what?
Polish Freedom Fighter. The Nazis
sterilised me. In rags and chains
I fled to Russia, eating snow
and crate-loads of stolen caviare,
weeping black salt. I was...what?
a small war hero, one medal only,
only a Jew in the Polish 2nd Corps.
I am...unlucky. I have no country
but that one; her name? what do they call her?'
'Marilyn. They call her Mandy.'

*

A chauffeur-driven Zis
eased from a mews entrance:
a chauffeur-driven Rolls
came in from behind.

A man called Lucky
pressed black seeds into Mandy's hand:
'Give these to Christine,
they're the stitches from my face.'

Babylon

The worm went round inside my head
when my brother left me,
his child in my belly;
I drove gold nails in the soft deal board,
brass nails into his bootprints, and the worm
went round the nails instead,
                              down
into masts of Ipswich pine,
Quebec Yellow, Yankee hackmatack,
round anchor-flukes and catheads,
under the crews in ticking jackets
and duck trousers with bloodied knees
from praying to the Star of the Sea,
drilling moonlight through binnacles,
down through transom and teak ballast,
lipped and peeling garboards
                              and down
into Brunel's imagination,
bursting out a million times its size
four-square on the mud and sewage
of St Mary's Rotherhithe.

                    *

'A wrack-survivor showed it me – oak spars
Valencienned by *Teredo navalis* –
I hired him on the spot. And the worm?
The worm modelled for my Patent Tunneller!'
In the violet light of the first banquet
under the Thames, the laughter of sixty angels.

   A cast-iron honeycomb seven yards tall
   furred with poling-screws, sixty working cells
   of navvies backed by brickies sealing
   the driving-spasms under a fontanelle
   of crushed gravel scooped like mother-of-pearl.

Brass plumes vaulted the gas candelabrum
from the band of the Coldstream Guards.
The sixty angels of the share certificate
fell among the oysters and champagne;
a toast brought Bandinel of the F.O.
waving that night's *Extraordinary Gazette.*

    The coffer dams scuttled, they shored from below
    lacing sacks of blue clay with hazel rods –
    still their sky leaked in; beads, brass money, gin-corks,
    a child's ivory teething-ring, water.

'Battle at Navarino! Arab Fleet Destroyed!
We will drive back the hordes of Islam
to where that dry creed drew breath and sword –
so here's to the wine of Melchizedek:
Down With Water and Down With The Prophet!'
Brunel squirmed with the history of it.

               *

    Where lingerest thou
    my Irish kind,
    over the water
    under the water?

        Wei
           le

                The arches bellied
                in the violet light
                like a knife testing
                a flank for entry.

                    wei
                      le

'I seed them Hirishers
tumblin' through the harches
screachin' Murther! Murther!
Out with them bloody lights!'

Waile!
Down by the river Saile
I wept for my damned sisters,
for pleasure-seekers
when the waters close,
for Trimmer Gorman, Cahillane
and all the nameless exiles,
Sligo, Semite, Vietnamese.
My brother's name is Babylon.

Dear Tsar Ferdinand

You are reading this to thirteen candles,
the March from *Aida* and Coptic spells –
I prefer *La Forza de Destino*
with Bulgar pigwidgeon. Madame de Thébes
promised you empery from Vienna
to Istanbul, but the porphyry slab
of the basileus will stay stone cold –
you should worry more about going bald.

Now my readings: *The Prophecy of Gifts*;
the two-headed viper work out for yourself,
but horned cockerels mean only world wars.
Don't eat them. *The Prophecy of Flowers*;
death within the Sobranie, Stamboloff
will fall apart before Turkish cutlasses.
His corpse will stink. Wear opera perfume
at the wake – choose the 'Violette de Parme'

I can smell now – and in your dress chain-mail
a Malmaison carnation just for me.
His hands will float in bowls of alcohol:
ensure they point only at the Exarch.
Avoid making jokes on the catafalque.
So much you've paid for, but on my name-day
I'm disposed to largesse in my helpings
with small confections of mille-feuilletons.

For your French blood: *Prophétie à la carte*.
Europe will dig in to Oeufs à la Turque,
Macédoine, your Faisan Bulgare au Blanc
with Sambuca and Crême Cardinal Serbe.
Your real choice concerns the dinner service;
Krupps or Maüser, Schneider-Creusot, Vickers –
dynasties hang on it. The closing strains
of *Aida* – catchy! Dear Tsar, bonne chance!

An Ontological Proof for the Existence of Ern Malley

Detective-Sergeant Jacobus Andries Vogelsang,
with vaseline in turmoil round his sand-cracked nostrils,
takes in the jury with his peripheral vision:
'It is immoral his use of the word "genitals"!'

There are millions of us in a dock designed for one
being charged with Offences Contra Bones Mores,
buttock-to-buttock like angels dancing on a pin.
Slippery with reason, I fly up from the sick rose

of poets folded by South Australian police,
past Mohammed's coffin, the floating Christ by Dali
to ERN'S CABARET, where Augustine the 'Potamus
is sand-dancing with Averrhoës the Dromedary.

A bird-headed jongleur in relaxes and gold tux
plays in *The Great Buggerall* (Ern) who grins, conjuring
hourglasses from my nostrils and cracking them like eggs.
'This holds up the weather,' he explains, 'I love the Spring.'

On the Atmospheric Road
(air)

There was Frank Elrington,
    sired by one of Dublin's Regius Professors,
investigating the front-
    motive carriage on the Samuda Brothers'
recently-installed atmospheric railway
    linking Kingstown with Dalkey
after a picnic one March morning
    in eighteen hundred and forty-three
and in the next instant he found himself
    breaking the world land speed record
while his accidentally-disconnected
    passenger-class vehicle
was inhaled at eighty-five miles per hour
    straight up a vacuum being abhorred
by the hundred-horse-power crank-overhead
    triple-Cornish pump and flywheel.

If there was a lesson in all this
    for Frank's countrymen of either sex
such as the need for 'absolute block' train-brakes
    or that engineering sucks,
it was lost on the rats who gnawed clean
    miles of pneumatic leather sausage
(made especially delicious
    by a cod-oil, tallow and beeswax fledge)
faster than engineers could replace them.
    Now all the engineers are dead
and the folklore and orature
    of the Dalkey rodent community
keeps strong a tradition in
    environmental-friendly technology
and takes a picnic once a year
    by the verge on the Atmospheric Road.

A World After Proverbs

'Where there is plenty, take plenty:
Where there is little, take it all.'

When the hour drew Motholoch to Rathlin,
breasting the signal from Marconi's ribs
in Ballycastle, she rode the Sea's Swallow
on a dulse raft towed by compass jellyfish.
They folded in the surf like tricolours
while she beached at the limbus of the moon
by logs furred with geese hungry to be born.

When she peeled the turf back from the mass-rock
it spoke to her of axe-makers and trade,
how oats and salt bought a corpse's gold teeth
or the silk taken from corpses, of fish
poisoned for the stories of three gold teeth.
'The oceans are poisoned now for nothing,'
she answered. 'The tooth-standard is still in force.'

When the Virgin folded in Rathlin surf
like a jellyfish, it gave the first sign.
From McFarland's abominable marriage
she took the next. Until the last seal breaks
Motholoch hunkers in the skulls of cars
scraping the bald patch on her fur with shells
which gossip of a world after proverbs.

Margin Prayer from an Ancient Psalter

Lord I know, and I know you know I know
this is a drudge's penance. Only dull scholars
or cowherds maddened with cow-watching
will ever read *The Grey Psalter of Antrim*.
I have copied it these thirteen years
waiting for the good bits – High King of the Roads,
are there any good bits in *The Grey Psalter of Antrim*?

(Text illegible here because of teeth-marks.)

It has the magic realism of an argumentum:
it has the narrative subtlety of the Calendar of Oengus;
it has the oblique wit of the Battle-Cathach of the O'Donnells;
it grips like the colophon to The Book of Durrow;
it deconstructs like a canon-table;
it makes St Jerome's Defence of his Vulgate look racy.
I would make a gift of it to Halfdane the Sacker
that he might use it to wipe his wide Danish arse.
Better its volumes intincted our cattle-trough
and cured poor Luke, my three-legged calf,
than sour my wit and spoil my calligraphy.
Luke! White Luke! Truer beast than Ciarán's Dun Cow!
You would rattle the abbot with your soft off-beats
butting his churns and licking salt from his armpits.
Luke, they flayed you, pumiced your skin to a wafer –
such a hide as King Tadhg might die under –
for pages I colour with ox-gall yellow...

(Text illegible here because of tear-stains.)

Oh Forgiving Christ of scribes and sinners
intercede for me with the jobbing abbot!
Get me re-assigned to something pagan
with sex and perhaps gratuitous violence
which I might deplore with insular majuscule
and illustrate with Mozarabic complexity
Ad maioram gloriam Dei et Hiberniae,
and lest you think I judge the book too harshly

from pride or a precious sensibility
I have arranged for a second opinion.
Tomorrow our surveyor, Ronan the Barbarian,
will read out loud as only he can read out loud
selected passages from this which I have scored
while marking out his new church in Killaney
in earshot of that well-versed man, King Suibhne...

(Text completely illegible from this point
because of lake-water damage and otter dung.)

NOTES

The Frog (page 14): In 1185 Giraldus Cambrensis paid his second visit to Ireland. During his stay a frog was found in Co. Waterford – a creature hitherto unknown on the island. The frog was brought before Duvenold, King of Ossory, who prophesied from it the enslavement of his country.

The Irish Slave (page 15): 'Corsairs raided the south coast of Ireland to punish the O'Driscolls, pirates themselves, who trespassed on Barbary hunting grounds' – Douglas Dunn, *New Statesman & Society*, 7 September 1990.

I'r Hen Iaith A'i Chaneuon (page 33): The title is Welsh and means 'To the Old Tongue and Its Songs'. The Irish translates roughly as: 'Speak not to me of the foreign prelate/ Nor of his creed with neither truth nor faith/ For the foundation stone of his temple/ Is the bollocks of King Henry VIII.'

The Bradford Count (page 36): The Bradford Count is a measure of fleece.

A Scarborough Warning (page 37): A Scarborough Warning is a Yorkshire idiom now meaning last warning, but originally no warning at all.

King of Infinite Space (page 40): The last line of this poem refers to the later version of Bismarck's celebrated disclaimer of German imperialist intentions.

Lumpenhund (page 47): Lumpenhund ('ragged dog') was the nickname of the youthful Richard Krebs, who wrote his autobiography describing his work as a double agent for OGPU with the Gestapo under the name of Jan Valtin.

A Café Waiter in Tel Aviv (page 50): The first line of this poem was the slogan of Russian immigrants to Nevei-Sherett (a Tel Aviv suburb), who rioted in 1972 at being housed too near Yemenite Jews.

A Squeeze (page 53): The Tailor and Ansty were an elderly couple in West Cork whose marvellous conversation was turned into a book by Eric Cross in 1942. In print their talk was too strong for the Censorship Board who banned it – three priests forced the Tailor to kneel and burn his own copy. In 1943 Sir John Keane, a Protestant landlord, tabled a motion in the Senate condemning the board for this decision but the division showed only himself and his reluctant seconder in favour.

Babylon (page 55): This poem is made from, among other things, two children's songs: 'Weile Weile Waile' is Irish and deals with infanticide and capital punishment, while 'The Bonny Banks of Fordy' is British and treats incest and suicide, and also supplies the last line.

Dear Tsar Ferdinand (page 58): Tsar Ferdinand of Bulgaria, like Hitler and Ronald Reagan, relied on astrologers for policy advice. The poem purports to be from one of his wise women.

An Ontological Proof for the Existence of Ern Malley (page 59): Ern Malley was an internationally known Australian poet of the 1940s whose fame was compounded by the prosecution of *Angry Penguins* (a literary magazine of the time) for obscenity in publishing his work. While in England some judges do not like the issue of guilt to trammel their exemplary sentencing, in Australia the trial went ahead despite the early disclosure in evidence that Ern Malley had never existed.